Fly High ✈
Soaring Amidst
Life's Turbulence

MiMi Q. Atkins

GLITTER MOON PRESS   GEORGIA   UNITED STATES

GLITTER MOON

Published by Glitter Moon Press
Stockbridge, GA 30281
www.glittermoonpress.com

ISBN-13: 978-0-9847473-4-4.
Library of Congress Cataloging–in-Publication Data.

Cover design: Adriannia Robinson
Interior Design: Dawnell Jacobs

Dedication

Daniel Joseph Monroe
"Chopper"
June 24, 1981 – November 1, 2006

You were my best friend and one of the most influential people in my life. You are the reason that I can not only fly, but soar. You gave me the wings to face my fears and you demonstrated love – one that will carry me a lifetime. I will never forget you and I will carry your legacy everywhere I go.

Acknowledgements

I am grateful for my family and close friends for encouraging and believing in me.

The essence of my life here on Earth, I owe to you my darling, Embry. To the world I may not mean much, but to you I am your world. You own the keys to my heart, my precious daughter and please know I do it all for you.

You are a faithful "frieditor" - Dawnell Jacobs. A friend and editor throughout my journey as an author. I can never repay for you the immense amount of love and support you have shown me over the years, so I won't try. Thank you for showing me the meaning of friendship.

Pastor Phillip Anthony Mitchell of Victory Church ATL, I thank you for all the sermons that were Holy Spirit filled and inspired me to "see beyond" "aggressively pursue," and to "be encouraged" over the past year. This book and many more will be tangible evidence to the messages you preached.

To anyone reading this book - may you always dare to dream and never cease to lose your sense of wonder.

Contents

Introduction

Life is like planning a trip and taking a flight. You conceive the idea of going to another place and you choose the route to get there. What you do and how you do it depends on who you are.

The airline you choose to fly with depends on the price or your brand loyalty. Some take the cheapest flight to save money, while others take business class for the comfort afforded and provided. The departure time you choose for your flight depends on how busy you are, or if you are a morning, afternoon, or evening person.

You pack and prepare for the trip's purpose - leisure or business or both, and you bring along the necessities. Then you make arrangements (I prefer an Uber) to get to the airport to board your flight. Depending on your trip, you arrive at domestic or international terminals to check your luggage, go through TSA for clearance and then you are free to roam or run to your boarding area for your flight. Pretty simple, right? The fun has just begun.

When you board the plane, unless it is a layover flight, all aboard have the same destination. You find your seat and prepare for takeoff. As the plane prepares to take off, it must wait for the signal and direction from air traffic control.

Once the direction is received, the pilot communicates with the passengers about takeoff time, the weather and its temperatures, and any possible delays. The engines idle and you wait in anticipation to be amongst the skies and then it happens, the engine roars louder and the plane rattles to ascension, your ears pop and suddenly you're 5,000 feet off the ground.

While in the air, the plane is met with resistance of the wind - turbulence. Turbulence is a violent and unsteady movement of air, water, or other fluid source. It threatens to make the plane descend and shake violently from side to side. In a soothing voice, the pilot comes over the intercom and announces his or her plans to navigate through the chaotic confusion of the winds, though the pilot can't do anything about turbulence because it's a force of nature humanity has no control over, they have the training to circumnavigate.

Guess what? Life has turbulence, also. In life turbulence acts as conflict or confusion, it is the force that threatens to tear your world apart which leads to tearing your life apart and breaking you down. Life's turbulence doesn't have to destroy you; you can use its force to strengthen and propel you forward.

Those issues that press you down and cause extreme alarm or panic - whether it be failing a test or class, a cheating spouse, revealing a health scare, enduring death, losing a job, buying a house, or being accused of something you did not do and facing trials in your home or community. I have endured turbulence and I want to share with you how to overcome it.

I am not perfect. Not even close. I am on a journey just like you are. Some days are awesome. Some days are terrible. I struggle every day, and though I don't know all the answers, I want to share what I do know that can impact your life and make it worth living despite the hard times.

While this book is not a cookie-cutter plan, it is my prayer that it gives you faith, hope, and love strong enough to endure life's trials. These are the seven principles that has fueled my life and helped me to soar in the midst of life's turbulence, and I hope in some way the words within resonate in your life and you walk away inspired, encouraged, and motivated to FLY HIGH.

Chapter One
Abounding in Faith

*"Now faith is the assurance of things
hoped for, the conviction
of things not seen."*
-Hebrews 11:1

aith is one of the biggest influences in our lives. For some it is our sole driving force in humanity and serves to shape our being. Faith defines some of the most defining moments in my life, for even when I had no words, it was the vehicle of faith that moved me.

Faith is a five-letter word that goes a long way. Faith sees the invisible and it still believes the unreachable is attainable. My faith stems from my beliefs in a higher power, and the higher power I believe in is God. I believe in a higher power when doing something outside of yourself because otherwise you will drown in your own humanity because of our human limitations and limited understanding of life and its occurrences.

Faith is what carried me in when I wanted to be carried out. The more I look at it, my entire life has been one big faith story waiting to evolve. Faith has allowed me to move to other states, travel to other countries, and do the unthinkable. I know it was faith because faith is bigger than me and I could never make some of the decisions I have made myself. Why? My fears usually triumph over my faith, but that all changed for me, recently.

***

A few months ago, I took one of the biggest plunges of faith in my life. I decided to follow my dreams and quit my seven-year teaching career. Why? I was no longer happy and I was miserable. The passion I had when I started teaching had fizzled. I would be in the classroom teaching and peer outside the window and feel like I was in prison. I no longer jumped with glee at the thought of teaching literature and grammar – I resented it.

I would sit in my car when I arrived to work and imagine being anywhere but there. Everything was different and nothing was the same. I wanted so desperately to own my own business, write books, spread love and hope to nation suffering from moral decay, and to travel the world doing missions work.

I prayed and fasted for weeks at a time for answers from God. I knew whatever this new phase was, it was going to be a spiritual move. Surprisingly, I got my answer while teaching F. Scott Fitzgerald's, *The Great Gatsby*, a great American novel whose theme is chasing and obtaining the American Dream. BOOM! It hit me. I chose to go to college because I did not have much growing up and I was always told higher learning was the route to go. I knew about the military and I had a certificate in Marketing from a technical school, but teaching was the more viable choice since I loved reading, or so I thought.

I soon realized I loved writing more than I love reading. I loved talking more than I loved teaching. I loved researching to build a business more than I loved researching to create lesson plans. I wanted to attend business meeting more than I wanted to attend faculty meetings.

In March of this year, I decided not to renew my contract as a teacher for the following year. I was ready to be an entrepreneur and writer. I was also ready to go into ministry full time. I was **READY!** After I turned in my resignation notice I did every dance known to man, and when summer arrived I had my itinerary planned. I was going to fulfill my dreams. I traveled to Arcahaie and Port Au Prince, Haiti for a weeklong mission trip, and then I went to Europe for two weeks. I dined and shopped in Brussels, Belgium and indulged in their popular chocolates. I danced and talked with the natives. I toured Paris, France and engulfed in as much of its culture as possible - even turning down two engagements (Frenchmen are enamored with American women per my experience), and I survived the airport attack in Istanbul, Turkey at Ataturk International Airport. I missed my flight to Rome, Italy, but I did not complain because I have faith that I will get to Rome in the very near future.

***

I have not always allowed my faith to lead me, and I do struggle with it at times now. For example, a week after I resigned I went to my boss and told her I made a mistake, only for her to tell me I was already replaced. Though I was sad momentarily, I knew I only asked for my job back because I was lacking faith. But the doubt and disbelief did not end there.

Two months after I quit teaching, I started doubting my new life as an entrepreneur, Bible teacher, and writer and I began to think maybe being a flight attendant could help me achieve my dreams of traveling and serving as a missionary, so I applied to be a flight attendant for a popular airline. I got not one but two rejection e-mails and it was then that I knew what God was telling me – keep the faith even when I can't see what He is doing.

***

Faith wavers because we are human. We house negative and positive emotions. It's important to realize that these emotions can be overcome with truth. Even though it gets hard for me at times and I can't see what is going on, I believe I am exactly where I need to be. And I cling to a snippet from a sermon my pastor, Philip Anthony Mitchell, preached a few weeks ago. He said, "A faith that is not tested is a faith that can't be trusted." This means God is with me as I endure this new journey and I need to continue forward in this phase of my life so I can be trusted with even bigger phases. Faith matures you and faith develops you.

I knew deep down inside I could not return to the classroom as a high school English teacher, as the passion had long died and was being replaced with a burning flame to be outside the walls - creating and inspiring others to live beyond the confines of the American Dream. I'd been suffocated by its demands long enough; it was time to be free and take flight to new territory.

Chapter 2
Giving and Receiving Love

*"I have decided to stick to love . . .
Hate is too great a burden to bear."*
-Martin Luther King, Jr.

ove is a decision and a choice. It is not a fleeting emotion displayed on television or movie screens. Love can compel you to see outside of yourself and inside of another person to help them become better. Love changes you. Love challenges you. Love is best understood from the actions it stimulates. Love reveals itself when it bears the weaknesses and failures of another; it alleviates the suffering of others as we fulfill the emotional and physical needs by humbly giving of ourselves.

Love does not cost anything and is not found in self-centeredness as it is a sacrifice. You can give without loving, but you can't love without giving. Sacrificial love does not follow feelings as they are temporal and love is deeper – it is eternal. Love requires that we give what we value most: our hearts, minds, souls, and strength – the things money can't buy.

***

I can attest to this. I fell in love for the first time when I was nineteen years old. My high school crush, Daniel Joseph Monroe and I reunited in the produce aisle in June of 2002 in Wal-Mart during our sophomore year in college. He and I had last seen one another at our high school graduation, so we had a lot of catching up to do.

We exchanged numbers with tomatoes and bell peppers as our witnesses and from the first phone call, we were inseparable. He was in college at Embry Riddle Aeronautical University in Daytona Beach, Florida. His major was Aeronautical Engineering and I was majoring in education at Darton College in Albany, GA.

Daniel was one of the sweetest men I have ever met. He was different and possessed such a zeal for life that left all who met him astounded. He was charmingly handsome, 6 feet tall, blue eyes, with blonde highlights in his brown hair. He looked like a surfer boy and I was smitten. He was the man all the women wanted and I was honored that I was the one he showcased on his arm. He equally admired me and treated me like a queen.

Besides his good looks, Daniel had the ability to teach others to live and love life. He would do extreme things like race his motorcycle and drag race his grey Ford Ranger truck. I was the nervous onlooker begging and pleading with him to not do his stunts because I feared he would get injured or even die. He would look me in the eyes and say, "MiMi, lighten up sweetheart; you have to learn to live and not be so fearful." Then he would lift my chin and kiss my forehead and head out to live life on the edge yet again.

Daniel's love changed me and transformed me over the few years we dated. I recall one warm day in June 2003, he took me to the regional airport in our hometown of Albany, Georgia and did not tell me why. I saw him talk with some of the staff and they then disappeared for ten minutes and Daniel came back with that Cheshire cat smile on his face. I knew then he was up to his usual shenanigans – mischievous acts.

"Why are you smiling like that?" I asked sheepishly as I gripped the chair because he was known for picking me up and carrying me off just to hear me scream at the top of my lungs.

"I have a surprise for you. Follow me," he said motioning to the door.

I followed him and he pointed to an airplane that was waiting outside. It was an older model plane and could sit four people.

"What are we about to do exactly?" I asked pensively.

"Since you have never been on a plane before and I know you are afraid of flying, I want to help you conquer that fear and I want to be your first and only pilot," he beamed as his blue eyes twinkled in the sunlight.

Even though I was afraid, I agreed to face my fears and trust Daniel to help me. I jumped in the plane, buckled the seat belt, and examined the plane from front to back. There were so many buttons and gadgets, and it was a small cramped space. I decided to be quiet and just enjoy this awesome surprise and amazing gift my super handsome boyfriend whom I was **NOW** madly in love with had planned for me.

Yes, I fell in love with Daniel that day. Not because of the gift or the act, but because he exemplified love. I began to see the power of love and how it transforms. Love means caring about someone and helping them to see the best in themselves. Love is not selfish and looking for an advantage over other people. Love is an action word and it evolves, inspires, and transforms lives.

Today, I am 34 years old and I have traveled internationally six times and I lost count of my national travels. What was my mode of travel? An airplane of course. I love flying now and I owe that to Daniel, and his desire to teach me to face my fears.

Daniel also taught me to face my fears of water by teaching me to swim in Daytona Beach. He was so patient, but I was too timid to even learn how to float, but he never gave up trying.

Sadly, Daniel died in 2006. He died doing what he loved most and fulfilling his dreams – teaching and flying. I admit I was afraid to fly for a few years after his death, but I know that he would never want me to be afraid of anything, and to keep his memory alive, I book flights and travel the world as frequently as I can with our darling daughter, Embry (you'll have to get our full story in another book).

***

Do you see what Daniel's love did to me? It influenced me to become fearless. It modeled to me another love besides my parent's love. While you don't have to see love from a romantic angle, you can embrace love from the angle of accepting people for who they are instead of who you want them to be.

Daniel also shared his passions with me because of his love for me. Imagine how you can ignite this world if you shared the things you loved with others. That is what our passions create within us – it creates a desire to share what we love.

I firmly believe the love I allowed myself to receive is the love I allow myself to give. Everyone wants to be loved and everyone needs love as it is what inspires us to continue when we want to quit – knowing someone cares enough for you and believes in you is endearing. It is the purest and most inexpensive gift we can give to those we encounter.

I am certain I am successful in business because I know how to love – which leads me to build rapport and relationships with people. I have a love for people that allows me to see them for who they are without judgement or constraints. I welcome new people into my world and provide them the opportunity to get to know me and me to know them.

Love's a four-letter word that could define and shake nations. A word that could give peace to our aching lands near and far. The word that could drive out hate if only people would allow it to permeate their hearts.

Love covers people when they make mistakes and aids in forgiving them while exercising wisdom and protecting yourself with boundaries. Love can heal the brokenness of this world, if we allow it, but it would require the transforming of heart, mind, and soul. We would have to reach the ugly places and deal with the grime deposited there for love to be the profound force it was meant to be for humanity.

Chapter Three
Loving and Embracing You

> *"Keep love in your heart.*
> *A life without it is like a sunless*
> *garden when the flowers are dead."*
> *– Oscar Wilde*

ou are your biggest fan in life, whether you acknowledge that or not. You are also, unfortunately your biggest critic.

Why? I am yet to figure this out, but a conversation with my daughter a few years ago gave me some insight into why we may be most critical of ourselves.

"Embry you are so beautiful to me,"

I said pulling her close so she could look into my eyes.

"Thank you, Mommy," she said looking bewildered while twisting her hair.

"You have the prettiest eyes," I continued while batting my eyelashes on her cheek.

As I pulled back from her I noticed a scoff on her face.

"Embry, why the long face?" I asked out of sheer confusion.

"Well, Mommy. I don't think I have pretty eyes," she started as I interrupted.

"You don't? What do you mean?"

"I see my eyes every day, Mom and they're green like pickles and pickles aren't a pretty green," she frowned as she pulled away from me.

I pulled her closer and pulled her face close to mine and whispered, "Don't see them as pickles then, see them as sparking emeralds. True beauty comes from within anyway."

She kissed my cheek, said thank you, laughed and ran away, but I sat in total silence for a few minutes reflecting on that conversation. My little girl, the one whom I adored and admired for always living so carefree had truly shocked me.

I loved her eyes, but since she had to live with them every day, she didn't see what I saw. I began to think about the way I see myself and how many times I could not see what other people would see in me, either.

***

I spent most of my life defining myself by my outward appearance because that is what the world defines us as – facial features, body type and weight, hair, etc. Those are superficial elements of personal identity and have nothing to do with the essence of who we are in regards to character. The world values reputation – what others think of you, while character matters most – who you really are.

I remind myself that I am different in most every aspect and that is not a bane – yet a gift. It is a gift to treasure and to behold and there is nothing wrong with marching to the beat of your own drum. Sadly, I was not always this way myself. I would look for affirmation in others – especially the men I dated and most times it ended in disappointment. I was looking for someone to tell me how great I was and not realizing greatness was already inside me. It was waiting for me to realize it and release it.

***

You are a vital part of your success. No, we don't have to be self-obsessed, but we can be humble and noble in our thoughts, actions, and deeds. Notice "YOU" are in the middle of faith and love in this book for without you, you will cease to exist. Your faith and your love are vital components to developing and shaping YOU.

Nothing in your life matters and can hold you down unless you allow it. If you harbor hate and a lack of belief in your life, it will fester and overcome who you are and cloud your vision from seeing the beauty in life. You will be challenged in every area in this journey called life and you can't avoid the trials and challenges as they serve to shape you – it all serves to help you become better.

I endured physical child abuse as a child. I was burned and beaten until I bled at times, so I have scars that serve to remind me of this hostile abuse. I did not hate the person who harmed me. I rose against them and sought to be better even though it was hard.

The sad thing is not many care about you and what you endure. It's all an excuse to them. Note, I did not say nobody cares – because there is always someone who does. You should care enough about you and understand you will always be with you, so not dealing with trials and pretending they do not exist only hurt and hinder you.

If I had allowed hate to permeate my being, then I would have never had a mindset to see beyond my trials. We must know we are not our situation and circumstances and embrace the differences we have as individuals.

Maybe you're different? People call

you weird? You're not weird or different – you are YOU. No two people are the same and cookie cutter just doesn't cut it. Why not stand apart because you do not blend in?

I knew I was called to be different. I never had a clique or a squad. I was unique enough to stand alone and cordial enough to be friends with everyone, but I liked being different. In fact, I love and embrace being unlike anyone else.

Being a teacher didn't take away my desire to be different either. I wanted to be free to be me – to break outside the walls of a traditional classroom and allow the world to become my classroom. I desire to inspire people to reach their goals and fulfill their dreams through perseverance. We need to be willing to accept and encourage one another and believe in one another for who they are and not what we want them to be.

Whenever I see someone pretending to be someone they're not, I cringe. I feel God did not create us to be a replica or a carbon copy of someone else. He made you unique and in your own image because you have your own route, journey, and destination.

***

I remember trying out for the basketball team in middle school because all the "cool" kids were doing it. I would go to practice every day and Mr. Templin (the coach) at Radium Springs Middle School would smile at me. I felt at any day he would cut me. Why? I sucked. I could not dribble to save my life, and now I realize what a fool I must have made of myself back then.

I recall when we had drills, Mr. Templin would blow his whistle and shout, "Atkins, you run as swift as a gazelle. Keep it up. I have my eyes on you."

That made my day. He did not focus on what I could not do; he focused on what I could do. That taught me a valuable lesson that I was not to learn until later.

You see, Mr. Templin knew leaders build. Leaders uplift. He knew if he yelled at me and told me I looked like an ostrich dribbling a ball, I would've ran to the locker room, stuffed my face in a locker and cried. Well, maybe not the dramatic parts, but I would've cried because I am very sensitive.

Also, what Mr. Templin did was give me a clue that I might be good at something else. So what I sucked at basketball? I could run the tar off a track. This and many more instances in life taught me the importance of being me and loving me for who I am, not who I am not.

Chapter Four
Desiring Hope

"Hope is the thing with feathers that perches in the soul - and sings the tunes without the words – and never stops at all."
– Emily Dickinson

ope is our greatest source when all else seems to be lost. Hope is a precursor to faith. While faith is trusting and believing in what you can't see, hope is imagining that there is something there to trust and believe in. Hope is the belief in the possible – what could be. It redefines probable and opens doors to the impossible. Faith is trusting God to help you, while hope is the pathway that considers there is a way for God to help you. Without hope, faith ceases to exist, because we can't ask for what our mind has not first conceived (imagined).

Hope is important because it allows us to face the difficulties and obstacles of life and increase our chances of success and achieving goals. Hope is important because it leads to faith even when we are lost.

***

I can recall a time in my life when I was extremely lost. The year was 2002 was one of the toughest years of my life. I was a total rebel and prodigal daughter. I experienced homelessness and had to live in my car, not because I had to but because of my pride.

One night in October 2002, I decided I was going to commit suicide. I was going to drive my car into something at top speed and prayerfully be killed by the impact. I lived in a small town and had no clue how I was going to do it, but I knew I wanted to end my life. So I drove and I drove. And I ended up at a building surrounded by three other buildings – one was Love. The others were Joy, Faith, and Hope. At the time, I was in love with a man who was slow to love me back, so I wanted desperately to land on those steps. The steps of love. As I prepared to walk to the steps, I saw a man and I began to follow him, or so I thought. I was crying out to him to help me as he was my last and only resort. No matter how much I cried and tried to catch up with him, I could not. I cried and I told God that I would keep going until I had no more energy and whatever steps I landed on – I would live my life in that way.

Broken, torn, and wet from my own tears – I opened my eyes to the step of hope. And I declared from that point on, that I would always have hope.

Three days later, I was at my university in our cafeteria and I happened to look at the ad board and a girl was looking for a roommate. I called her to inquire and she ended up being an old middle school friend. She allowed me to move in that night. Instantly, my prayers for housing was secured and answered. I remember going outside and looking up at the sky, thanking God. He'd delivered me and saved me from killing myself and I now had hope – hope that I would carry with me then and still carry with me now.

Chapter Five
Creating Innovation

"You have to have a big vision and take very small steps to get there. You have to be humble as you execute but visionary and gigantic in terms of your aspiration. In the Internet industry, it's not about grand innovation, it's about a lot of little innovations: every day, every week, every month, making something a little bit better."
– Jason Calacanis

*I*nnovation doesn't necessarily involve an invention; it can be birthed from life's rejection. While creating a novel product or service is innovative, creation can also spawn from the imagination in other ways and can be adapted by others.

Since elementary school, I have been awarded for the projects and ideas I created. I was always the one thinking outside of the box because I liked being different and unique. Unfortunately, as an adult everyone does not embrace my creativity and I have faced many rejection and hardships.

***

I wanted to become published in the Christian romance arena, so I would submit to literary agents and publishers, only to get rejected. One day, I used my nickname "MiMi" instead of my birth name, "Miesha." And guess what happened? I had more leads. Some of the companies who rejected me before would keep my manuscript in case they were interested in the future. This was when I used MiMi, yet they blatantly rejected "Miesha." How was this so?

It was then I realized I was being discriminated against because of my name which in tune meant my race. I was livid. I began to wonder if those companies even read my manuscript.

So, I decided to fight back in the best way. I started *Glitter Moon Press*, my own publishing company, because I was tired of "No," and I wanted a "Yes." I promised I would never discriminate against a person's work/worth in light of their talent. And I wanted to extend the opportunity to others to help them get published and to assist them in the total process.

My business is not just for me; it's to help other writers and authors hold their book(s) in their hand and see them smile. I created a business because I did not like nor accept the rejection I faced.

Innovation drove me to create my own publishing business, though that is not the only business I created from innovation. I created *Cheritees*, an apparel and merchandise brand for entrepreneurs and creatives because I discovered there was not many existing businesses that honed into this sect of people. The sad thing is I had no idea I created the idea as I was simply creating graphic t-shirt designs and the digital strategist recommended I market entrepreneurs. As you can see, novel ideas oftentimes aren't so novel.

If you are a creative, I advise you to continue to create because in you lies some form of business or creation that you can share with the world that we can benefit from and that can make you money. Innovation starts from within – one clever idea at a time.

Chapter Six
Setting and Achieving Goals

"Desire is the key to motivation, but it's determination and commitment to an unrelenting pursuit of your goal - a commitment to excellence - that will enable you to attain the success you seek."
– Mario Andretti

oals are the aims of achievement with the expectation of a desired result. When was the last time you set a goal? Did you achieve it? What is the number one reason you don't achieve goals? A lack of motivation.

Though a lack of motivation is the main reason we struggle with achieving our goals, goal setting is important and can help with motivation.

When you set goals, it provides a long-term vision for short-term motivation. Goal setting helps you organize your time and your resources as you focus on knowledge acquisition. Goals boosts your self-esteem and confidence, as well as motivate you depending on the simplicity and complexity of the goal.

A simple goal involves a short process and does not require much time. It does require motivation. For example, eating three healthy meals a day is simple as it requires you to buy the ingredients and make the meal. Although, for someone who struggles with their diet or consistency, this could be a complex goal.

A complex goal is similar to a long-term goal, and it involves many steps and often times other agents to achieving it. Planning a wedding is a complex goal because it involves several other people, and even though you can plan a wedding in a short amount of time, dealing with people will always result in some form of complexities, chaos, and challenges.

Setting goals means knowing your limits and boundaries. You know yourself and your abilities best. Don't allow others to set goals for you or aspire to achieve the goals of others – comparison is the biggest goal and dream killer in life, so it is imperative you stay in your own "goal" lane.

***

I set goals all the time and many times I am not successful at achieving them because I set them on a whim or out of emotion. I also struggle with organizing my goals on paper as I am a mental organizer; I keep a lot of things in my head. That may seem impossible to conceive or believe because I was once a teacher and even more unbelievable because I am an entrepreneur and a writer, but it is my truth. I am working on improving the way I set my goals and master them because at times I can become overwhelmed because I am an optimist and once I envision something I try to carry it to fruition.

One goal I set was to graduate from PhD school within four years, but I had an incident to occur (death in the family) during my last year, which caused me to turn in an assignment late and I was not allowed to resubmit. I was only a dissertation away from becoming Dr. Atkins and the dream was deferred. I was hurt initially, but then realized I only wanted a PhD because it was the "American Dream" and it never was an ideal goal or dream of mine to have.

The goals and dreams I have set for myself now involve missions. I want to do missionary work in at least three countries over the next three years. I had the pleasure of doing missions in Haiti this past summer and it changed my life tremendously. I was able to embrace the Haitian culture and still cling to my own and develop a love for the people and their customs and beliefs, so I am certain I would benefit much from future missions trips.

Another goal I have set for myself is to sell over 20,000 books within the next year so I can fund those mission trips and to eventually plant schools in areas that are dear to my heart – Ethiopia and Haiti. I firmly believe education holds the key to many opportunities and I would love to help other children learn.

This book will make my dreams possible, as well. I plan to travel the world as a motivational speaker, sharing my story of how I survived a once destitute life and gained a college education despite the odds stacked against me. I will encourage the world to "Fly High" despite the turbulent winds life may blow our way.

Chapter Seven
Accepting Help

*"We are all here on earth to help others;
what on earth the others are here
for I don't know."*
– W. H. Auden

H elp is a person's way of extending their hearts outside of their bodies, and if you are like me you don't accept help easily or in most situations and circumstances. I think part of my reason for dismissing help is how I was raised. My mother and father always told us to "make a way" as children and that usually meant not asking for help and figuring it out on your own. I can see where this trait made me extremely innovative, but I can see where it has made me suffer in areas where I could build or improve a relationship.

Many see asking for help as a sign of weakness when in actuality it is a strength and can help build your character. While it may sound modest enough, accepting help is something that is extremely challenging most of us at some point in our lives. It can be extremely problematic for those of us who believe that seeking help undermines our independence and our ability to cope. However, by rejecting help, we disregard the essential fact that we are social beings who need to communicate and cooperate with one another in order to prosper. It's possible to change your thinking and become more receptive to help in the future.

We all need help. It seems we don't at times and pride will get the best of us.

We've heard the cliché "no man is an island," and it's true. Surround yourself with helpful people who won't boast or mock your needs. The people you surround yourself with will have an impact on you. We need people around us to challenge us in all aspects of our lives, so don't allow pride to have you reject help from others.

Surround yourself with people who will hold you accountable not people who will coddle everything you do. People who always praise you and never correct you are not necessarily good. We need truthful people in our lives

Speaking of help, I hope in some way the contents of this book has helped you. Now that you have finished this book, please go back and look at the bolded first letters in each chapter. Did you see the creative and innovative (there's those words again) effect? How *innovative*, right? They form **FLY HIGH**.

That's right, you've been flying high the entire time you've been reading this book:

Faith
Love
You
Hope
Innovation
Goals
Help

Those key principles have helped me soar amidst life's turbulence, and they can help you, too. You are now equipped with tools to help you grasp your goals and cling to inspiration.

Fly High by abounding in faith, giving and receiving love, loving and embracing YOU, desiring hope, creating innovation, setting and achieving goals, and accepting help.

About the Author

MiMi A. Atkins is the best-selling author of *From Bossed to Boss: 10 Lessons Entrepreneurship Has Taught Me* and *So, You Want To Be An Entrepreneur? Planning, Building, and Sustaining Your Business*. She is the CEO and designer of *Cheritees*, a brand of lifestyle apparel for entrepreneurs and creatives, FoundHER of *cHERish*, Inc., a non-profit organization for women desiring Biblical womanhood, and the CEO of *Glitter Moon Press*, a publishing imprint for authors.

MiMi lives in Atlanta, Georgia and enjoys homeschooling and traveling the world with her daughter, writing fiction and non-fiction, speaking and teaching, and serving as a missionary and lover of orphans. MiMi is currently writing her first fiction novel - an inspirational romance entitled, *3627*. It is set to debut Winter 2017.

Need a Motivational Speaker?

Book *MiMi.*

Contact MiMi Q. Atkins at the following:

- ✓ *www.glittermoonpress.com* for publishing information.
- ✓ *www.mimiqatkins.com* to book MiMi for church events.
- ✓ *www.shopcheritees.com* to shop or book MiMi for Fly High.
- ✓ *www.thecherishspot.org* to join other women for sound doctrine.

Available Now!